What Nature Really Tells Me

Gary Frederic

Published 2023

Printed in the United States of America

First Edition
ISBN (print): 978-1-963380-00-2
ISBN (e-book): 978-1-963380-01-9

For information, address:
Holzer Books LLC
8 The Green, Ste. A
Dover, Delaware 19901 USA

For information about special discounts available for bulk purchases, sales promotions, and educational needs, contact:
info@holzerbooksllc.com
+1 (888) 901-7776

Scripture quotations are taken from the New World Translation of The Holy Scriptures (2013 Revision), published by Jehovah's Witnesses.

holzerbooksLLC©

TABLE OF CONTENTS

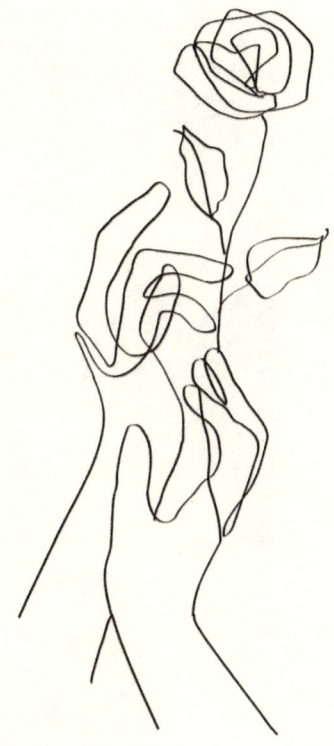

GARY FREDERIC

A Striking Stag

The alpha male is robust.
He's decked out;
looking sharp with his tawny suit,
marching like a king with his crown;
searching the dance floor to find his queen.
He's on the prowl!
Her moisture has reached his atmosphere;
He spots the girl.
He is closing in on her sweet perfume;
He grabs her hand for a dance.
The music starts as they latch on & move as one;
Checkmate!

GARY FREDERIC

Autumn Blankets Fall

We feel good inside when these **leaves** die,
Because the changes made, colors them differently.
Then they **fall** like **embers** from the **sky**.
Some think this is a mystery.
But this transformation was designed,
To leave an impression on the heart and mind.
Look! They've got us in a trance!
The heart is commanded to be in a stance.
Instead of staying up, they shoot down like little **flares**.
All the while, colorful joys they share.
They carpet the **ground** and give us an anklet.
They huddle together to form a blanket.
Autumn *blankets* **Fall**,
They know and hear **winter's** call.
If you feel cold inside,
This is a good comforter under which to hide!
Thank Jehovah for this coming **Fall**,
For He has once again made it wonderful for all!

Autumn is My Favorite Season in This Museum

Autumn is my favorite season in this **museum**;
In this portrait, clearly – you see **Him**!
To me it's the most expensive piece.
It comes to my home every year!
It's not mine, so I'm on a lease.
Autumn is a world traveler, so it doesn't stay
When it goes on display, I will be a stowaway
There's only one charge for this fare;
So, people from everywhere follow to stare.
They hear the call.
This is the **Gold Rush**!
It's the mink coat for **Fall**
Artwork that always make us blush
As the Sun glazes on these trees it looks like **honey**;
Something special which costs no money
As if it's mining in my secret place,
These colors make my heart detonate!
Without making a sound, inside me **Autumn** resonates.
Because it's my favorite piece,
I always want to renew my lease.

Autumn Lights Fall

In **Autumn** the sun makes candles that light during the day.
We marvel at these colors even though it's not the month of May.
They surround us as if producing a show;
With help from the sun, their colors are saying: **'Action – Glow!'**
Autumn will light **Fall**,
And, to our hearts will go out the call:
Look! In Jehovah, we have to boast!
Because he's transforming things again on this coast.
We cannot paint these leaves like him,
But our hearts with admiration we can fill to the brim!
Look! **Autumn** will light **Fall**!
Even when they fall, their glow will not stall.
Like embers, they say goodbye to us.
They still capture our attention although making no fuss.
Like little flashlights they seem to light up.
In addition, they burn without getting hot.
Another Miracle to marvel at, and store in our heart's cup.
For Jehovah's works will forever hit this spot.
Because **Autumn** will produce falling lights this season,
Makes added *Praise to Jehovah* a great reason.

Autumn Rains Fall

Our prescription is to take a daily dose,
Walk along and examine them close.
Autumn Rains Fall
Before they drop, they call.
These **leaves** transform like art.
These colors go down deep into the heart!
In style, they say goodbye to us as they part.
They neither sing nor talk;
But like lit troops they go out.
Their mission: don't fall until we're taught
To capture our attention, their colors shout:
Autumn Reigns Fall!

Autumn will Make my Rug

Autumn is this month's fabric;
From these **leaves** my rug will be woven.
Though this material feels like plastic,
They are given free and never stolen!
These colors are the perfect pattern!
They look like wool that's on fire but never burns;
For the day they guide like a lantern.
It seems like a design we naturally yearn.
Autumn will make my rug.
When I'm outside in the **Fall**,
Autumn will give me a hug.
I will window shop in this Mall.
Autumn will make my rug!

Can I Paddle and Swim in this Ocean?

O Jehovah, I sit in front of an ocean
that is vast and deep, having no end in sight.
If I used a canoe and paddled out there,
would you watch over me?
Yes, it would be hard work;
but I want it to be, not in a boat nor in a ship.
I want to paddle and swim in **this** ocean.
O Jehovah, I know that it would be an endless experience,
but in the **vast ocean of your thoughts** I don't mind being lost.
Teach me how to swim in these deep waters.
If these currents take me out too far,
reel me back in; be my sail and anchor.
Tell me when to jump in, and when not to swim.
Would you be my lighthouse?
You give light; you gave us the sun, stars and the moon
to direct us on these wide moving waters.
O Jah, even to some of the birds you gave ability
to dive deep into these waters so that they may find their food.
If I tried to plunge in like them,
would you give me goggles and a snorkel
so that I can see in this deep watery place?
If I had fins, would you let me swim in your thoughts?
Let me paddle in a canoe during the sunset,
and let me swim during the sunrise.
O Jah, Jehovah my God, can I paddle and swim in this ocean?
If you permit, please remember, to keep your eyes on me;
Because I can drown in this vast space.

O Jehovah, how true the inspired words found at ***Romans 11:33:*** *"O the depth of God's riches and wisdom and knowledge! How unsearchable his judgments are and beyond tracing out his ways are!"*

GARY FREDERIC

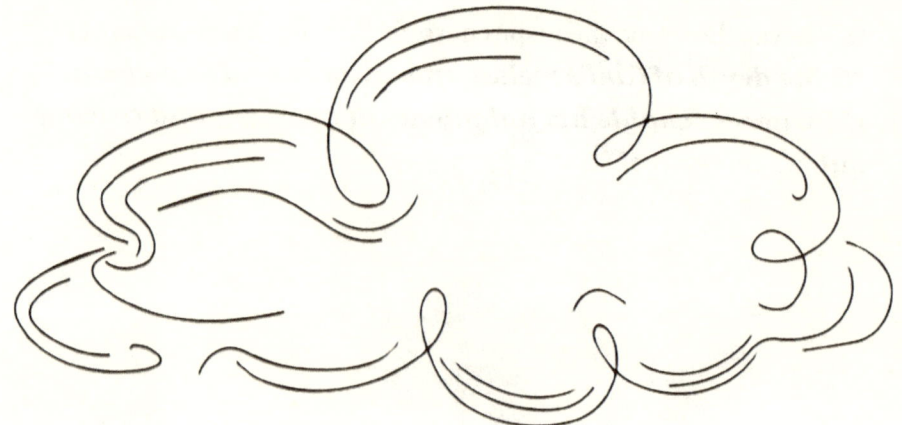

Clouds

You go where you want
    You look down at us laughing as you taunt
    When it is warm, you stand up like dry cotton balls
        When it is cold you resemble floating Marsh mellows
        When you cry everyone will know
            When you sigh & puff we feel it as the winds blow
            When you're in labor snow falls
                When you're not home the sky is blue
                When you're angry we hear the sounds of thunder
            Sometimes, like you, we'd wish we flew
            But still yet, we're always amazed at this wonder
        And we ask: *'How do you float?'*
        You reside over land, and the places made for boats
    Even planes need permission to enter your space
    The birds laugh at us because you've made them your friends
They are the only ones you let see your face
Because they're carrying the messages you send
    There's only One who can capture you with a rope
    To lead you to his palace to fill his moat
        "Who put wisdom into the clouds"? – JOB 38:36
        "The One who covers the heavens with the clouds" – PSALM 147:8
"He causes clouds to ascend from the ends of the earth." – PSALM 135:7

COVID-19 Stars

Some stars were made to be seen in the skies,
Others were made to be in the seas.
And then there are those made for the heart.
Some we see shooting from space,
Others are on shore because of being misplaced.
Then there are those born for problems we face.
Some are noticed only when they part,
And others when their comfort starts.
But they all give the heart a spark.
Some stars are seen,
Others are only spoken of by word.
But they all right now beam,
As their work on life is heard.
This is a season for Doctors EMT's & Nurses to shine!
For their work is precious,
Especially to the life of mine!
My wife is also a nurse,
So I know you're making a sacrifice that hurts!
Either way, they're imitating **Jehovah**, the **God** above,
Who sent to redeem us by the son of his love.

Fall Once More

The strokes of this Painter we most certainly adore,
    As **Autumn** between those **colors** sore.
    His hand will make art,
    Portraits that will reach the heart!
        All we have to do is watch and admire,
        So that we may learn and let love fire.
            What we have inside is already burning,
            Because his work, though simple is already turning.
                For what's happening hits the core.
                Let it **Fall** once more!
                It's **Autumn** again,
            A season with **coffee** blends.
    Fall once more – **Autumn**,
        And praise this Maker – who as a painter is Awesome!
    Yet, this season, **Fall** Once More!
    "be joyful and rejoice in Jehovah your God;
For he will give you the Autumn rain in the right amount." – JOEL 2:23
Try as you may, those **leaves** falling, you won't be able to count!
    Just praise our Creator by sounding your horn!
        Because something else will fall to the ground,
            It's inconspicuous and called the **acorn**.
    Though not as **colorful** as the **leaf**, it will fall with a greater sound!
        So enjoy what you see and hear again this **Autumn**,
            As they both **Fall** Once More

Fall South Like Monarch Butterflies

The leaves will Fall south like monarch butterflies.
During the day, they will decorate the skies.
They will transform to mesmerize!
And for Autumn, these will become a spectacle.
Because it's a season that's exceptional,
Their performance will be a festival!
Just take out the heart's lens and have a seat,
And enjoy the moment with a treat.

Favor Fall Forever

From flower fashions,
Fade Fastens.
Fingers feel Flutes;
Falls first Fire fruits.
Fuse frames,
For favorite flames.
Fiji file for future flight;
Falls fame forever fights!
Flee Fireflies,
Flee freshwater fallfish,
Forest Fireworks fly!
Free fighting fists,
Farmers & Firefighters film
Famous fire-fabric fills,
Flowers free from fetters.
Forecast, fog -foo,
Few feathers
Falcons farther Flew
Favor Fall Forever!

GARY FREDERIC

For My Vase She Blossoms

With a curative smile,
to amend my bliss
she blossoms vigorously

Flowering gracefully
she matures with an amiable atmosphere
having a delicate taste which is lucrative to my soul

She opens up with a gentle tone
I will call her a gardenia,
with a glabrous coat

Though mild & inconspicuous,
she glares humorously
As the sun on her shines,
to reveal a burst of brilliance

For my bosom she erupts,
with a genuine translucent color painted like a rainbow
Freely she flourishes,
for my vase she blossoms

Foxy Fall

This **fox** wears **Autumn** well
With a tip toe dance in **Fall**,
Her garment has me derailed!
With these rustic colors she blends;
Among the **Fall** colors she tends.
Like these **leaves** she reaches my hiding place and gives me food,
Transforming the effects on my mood.
She dances in the **leaves**.
And, although these **leaves** are dying, we don't grieve,
Because **Foxy *Fall*** brings joy.
For these leaves reign and don't annoy.

Hosting Fawns

Our two new neighbors were the cutest things;
They were the two **fawns** that took this Spring!
Their mother daily left them as our guests till the end of Summer.
We watched them grow to be good runners.
For hours they made our backyard their bed;
As they got to know us, they would lie quietly and just turn their heads.
Though the air conditioner became their favorite music box,
Only uninvited guests would make them hop.
Because our place became their favorite **lawn**,
These were the only guests welcomed before **dawn**.
They got to know our place very well.
These two **fawns** had us in a spell.
Since the **doe** learned of this place from her own mother;
When these **fawns** grow up & have their own, we hope they bring others.
We're now advertising a free AirBnB for hosting *fawns*.
Their **bed and breakfast** is our **lawn**.
Our **price** is just the benefits of watching & learning from our guests;
These dividends are most certainly the best!

I Love to Fall in Love with Fall

I love to fall in love with **Fall**!
Autumn, please stall...
Like a beautiful tapestry you are even seen from space;
You're colorfully painted in Autumn for green to replace.
Jehovah starts on a green canvas,
And when finished, it becomes Autumn's crown.
It even serves as therapy for the anxious,
Taking away the frown.
Like a stoplight you tell our hearts to *slow* down
To look at strokes from a great Artist who paints as he pleases.
When the Sun shines on these **Autumn** leaves,
Their colors resemble lights that twinkle and with the wind row.
Hello **Autumn**, speak to the heart and make things flow!
I wish **Autumn** could stall;
Because I love to fall in love with **Fall**!

It Will Fall Again

Prepare your eyes,
And open wide your heart.
Jehovah's about to mesmerize,
With his wonderful art.
Just capture the moment.
Because though short-lived,
He prepares it for our enjoyment.
You'll be glad of what it gives!
For it won't be the same.
Each one is new,
And always cheerful it came.
It will **Fall** again.
The season of **Autumn** reigns!
Gleefully shining its leaves,
To announce the coming Winter breeze.
It will **Fall** again.
As **Summer** comes to end.
Look! It's the **leaves** last dance,
And the moment of trance.
It will **Fall** again!
Snap every shot with your eyes,
Capture it with the heart's lens!
Behind the scenes, keep the **skies**,
Before this moment ends.
Because it will **Fall** again!

Jardin D'Amour: Sight

"MY SISTER, MY BRIDE, IS LIKE A LOCKED GARDEN, A SPRING SEALED SHUT." – SONG OF SOLOMON 4:12

She is a well cultivated region
A daughter of innumerable delights
Her likeness is as an apple tree
She is like a basket of fresh picked apples from paradise
Her adulation for the true God has caused her to be a magnificent glow
She is ablaze & flaming awesome as a forest fire
Yes, like a dancing flame surrounded by the wind, she swiftly runs with summer
Her teeth are a glow of pearl white, being my moon when she smiles
In her sandals her feet are like sweet spices
Her stem is dressed with a sleek tone of love
She is a flowering gem whose residence is in her Gardener's house
Her lustrous beauty is an apple tree of delight,
Under which there will be an approach for shade
She is a blossom of lilies adorned in spring
Her legs are dazzling,
Fashioned in a pattern of slender stems and are as healthy elongated sugar canes
She is one meticulously crafted by Jehovah
For this reason her artful design has blossomed triumphantly

Jardin D'Amour: Scent

"AWAKE, O NORTH WIND; COME IN, O SOUTH WIND. BREATHE UPON MY GARDEN. LET ITS FRAGRANCE SPREAD." – SONG OF SOLOMON 4:16

Her tone is watered with a gentle breeze,

Which saturates her to be a welcome of dandy-lions

Her air is scented with lilies

Her breath is scented like a bloom of roses

Her speech is a blossom of wild flowers

In her Bosom, there is found a chamber of sweet incense and love

She opens in the evening with a Jasmine-like scent,

To be the most fragrant of blooms

Accompanied with the sunset, she is a colorful breeze awakening dawn

Her petals are of the finest oils

To my nose this flower garden is of the sweetest smells

For indeed this love is from above fell

GARY FREDERIC

ardin D'Amour: Touch

"YOUR SHOOTS ARE A PARADISE OF POMEGRANATES. WITH THE CHOICEST
FRUITS, WITH HENNA ALONG WITH SPIKENARD PLANTS."
- SONG OF SOLOMON 4:13

Look! The honey bees have come out,
As her nectar is both sweet & rich
A garden barred in is my sister,
But because I have the key she will open up to me
She is risen up as a delicious fruit
She is a basket of luscious fruits that I will warmly embrace
In her orchards I have found delightful eats
For her fruits there is a stampede of flames marching like the blooms of the saffron
She is a cluster of sweet raisins
As one pleasurable to my palate she is as the taste of Kiwi fruit
Small, delicate & tasteful
This modest lily is a stream of precious spices
With my garden I will spend the night
As with the enjoyment of a watermelon, so will my cherished one be
Her fruits I will cherish, her heart I will meld with mine
And together for our enjoyment we will pick grapes to make wine

GARY FREDERIC

Let the Moon Come Down

Open your hand, O Jehovah
Release the joy, and reveal your love
Pull the tides of my heart,
And cause its seas to part
Implant your glow,
and allow your love to flow
Open your hand
Let the moon come down
I will catch it by the shoreline as I stand
I won't let it fall
For you, I am standing tall
You know, for your eyes have seen
it opened the innermost part of me, and within it you screened
Now, please, open your hand, O Jehovah,
for my heart is open to you
And its tides have become agitated on account of your love
Look! The sand and I; we are one
But my heart has stationed you above
Let the moon come down, O Jehovah,
and let it be your will done
You gave this pearl to us
It was in your wisdom that you made art,
and your way to move & please the heart
Its waves & its tides are racing and searching for Jehovah – its Maker
Open your hand, O Jehovah
Let the moon come down
Let it glow
And let your love within flow
Forever & ever
Amen.

Lily Chic

Sweet innocence blossoms during the nighttime splendor
Avoiding the lucrative atmosphere when day is adorned with the morning glory
She opens with soft and gentle skin that reveals a touch of tender
Her growth has captured my senses; and now I have made request to be told her story
Her bodyguards are the bees
They hum a song acquainting you with the stings that screen her picture
And she rewards them with an aromatic mixture
Adorned in a trumpet skirt of brown
She wears a soft golden splendor crown
Above her, hovers a cloud that spreads a watering net
To saturate and make a flavorful wet
From her succulent stems sprout a gorgeous bloom
Wherein lie the heavily scented oils from her interior room
A door is open; for her odorous scent drifts
An aromatic scent now rains from the sky
My visit was accidental, but my escape is a swift retreat
With my head down I turn to the roses and say hello
And the other flowers I wave to greet
Then I exit the garden to return to my desert terrain

Luminosity

O Moon, who can stop your light of passion?
Even the oceans, they clap and they applaud you.
When you are full, like a pearl you adorn the night sky.
Your moment is made for dominating the night.
When you are asleep the waters will speak for you.
When your eyes start to open, you peak at us like a crescent.
When you stare, you appear as the largest Pearl ever seen!
When you're laughing no one knows.
When you try to hide behind the clouds, they see you and they flee.
Your shadow you cast on the seas that they may plea.
When you speak, the oceans amplify your voice.
Let the moon come down, as the waves perform their show.
Let the waters dance, and let them congratulate you, O Moon!
Are you not the bosom buddy of the earth?
Wherever our earth travels, you follow because you are its bride!
Like a beaming eye you look down at night.
Even when you're asleep you reassure us that you're still around;
The tides and waves you command to give off your welcoming sound.
Your stage was made for the night;
and your catwalk is for our earth only.
The show you put on is like no other.
Luminosity.

Moving Wrinkles

How long have you been trying to run onto land,

And how long have you been trying to cover the sand?

So that we may not know the age of these seas, you gave them moving wrinkles.

Whether it is night or day, they never tire of greeting the coastlines!

Because they cannot enter beyond the limits you gave them, they moan.

But when they taste the boundary you set, their happiness is seen when they foam.

Their voice is heard day and night as they rush in against their borders.

Even when calmly asleep, they respect your orders.

You gave them moving wrinkles on their face.

So that we may not be able to know their age.

And you gave them power that is needed to win their race.

You even tamed them so that man can float on this moving stage.

To the seas you gave moving wrinkles,

So that whether it be a whale,

Or a mighty ship that sails,

Even these wouldn't stand out like a dimple.

Not even the things inside that call you home knows.

The two you gave authority over them continue to laugh.

Because they control the direction they flow,

The Sun and Moon we see smiling as they use you as their mirror.

Then we have to remember as we see this marvelous show,

All we have to do is continue to praise Jehovah as our Creator more clearer.

My Drown Deep Experience

These are the only waters that I don't mind drowning in;
Where I won't call out to be rescued,
A place where even though I get lost and can't find my way,
My direction I'd find pleasure in taking all the time in the world to locate.
For I'm in no hurry to get out of this place.
In fact, even though this ocean is vast and the deepest of all waters,
Just give me a snorkel for my survival.
While I go down, and drown,
Let me explore and explore before taking my last breath.
And what shall I say about this insatiable desire?
It was made to be satisfied!
My only regrets, although I love bathing in this aquatic place;
These waters are too clean and pure for me,
As I see my reflection every time I jump in for a dip.
But when I come up,
I'd still dry off without a towel to savor the moment.
I'd watch as each droplet of water rolled off my skin,
Even trying to count them as they drop.
What power these streams have;
For I feel the waves even in my heart!
What more can I say, for the joy this experience gives from you wetting me like this?
Only, Thank you, Jehovah, my God!
For allowing me to get soaked in these Deep waters, your living Word, The Bible!

Season of Dry Flames

With an introduction of **leaves** that appear to ignite,
Autumn returns with its **dry flames**.
Because they animate, electrify and excite,
O Jah, Jehovah, our hearts your works do claim!
For every heart wishes to be its aim.
And because this season is fixed,
It will always bring a colorful mix!
A season with **dry flames**.
It will never be extinguished,
Because its fuel is from a natural source.
It will burn for a moment,
Because with winter it will make an elopement,
To sleep and change its course.
But then it will return,
Resembling a fire that coldly burns.
It is here to teach,
So that we can make little **flames**
To warm ourselves when **cold**
And the **freeze** to partially tame.
With the same wood our small torches hold.
In a beautiful way we're being taught!
By the Season of **Dry Flames**,
Our Maker has our hearts caught.
Attention these colors of **Autumn** do command,
A gift made anew by this Artist's great hand!
They all resemble colorful flames that burn even when wet,
And they decorate everywhere until the sun sets.
The season of **Dry Flames**!
Praise Jah, because **Autumn** reigns!

She is an Ocean of Love

With permission to swim,
I will dive in these waters to claim my prize!
The calmness of the tides I will rip,
To explore the depth of my waters.
The heart of this sea will be mine;
It will be my domain to surf.
It is ever clear as crystal,
Clean and pure.
Indeed, in this ocean I *will* find satisfaction!
The sun will set and the moon will rise,
And my sea breeze will come;
With a calm heart she will drift my way
And to my ocean of love I will go
I will drown deep in her love,
To find the freshest fish in her bosom,
For she is my Ocean of love.

GARY FREDERIC

Spring Sings!

Spring's singing: 'Stop **sleet** & **snow**;
Spark & sling, Summer sow!'
Sweet scents & sounds saddle senses.
Sunsets & sleep spoil,
So sunrise seeks & soaks **soil**.
Stay & say something sweet;
Sacrifice **seeds** & speak!
Sing Spring, sing!
Share smiles,
Sleek styles!
Sea soaks sandals & **sand**;
Sun & success stands.
Sing Spring, sing!
Say something smart;
Slaying somber starts!
Savor some **Starbucks** & sunrises;
Set soles & sample superlative surprises.
See stuff sprout!
Say something – shout:
Spring sings!

The Leaves Leave a Leaf

The Leaves will leave a leaf.
So few that trees will resemble a reef.
Before they die, something must stick,
Changes are seen – Green, orange, yellow then rustic.
The heart will smile,
Because Autumn will reign for awhile.
These leaves will age with grace,
As the sun's glory reflects on their face.
Autumn will be seen for miles,
And leaves will Fall in style.
Even visitors want to stay!
For such a show, what price can we pay?
It's free, and our hearts will always be won!
Front row seats for everyone.
The leaves will leave a leaf
A reminder that this theatre will play again.
And this show will always win!

The Moon is Lit

In the stillness of the night there's an ethereal quality.
It's a motionless air that still speaks in quietness.
The moon's target is the heart; bullseye marks it's spot!
Stopping by, it shows hospitality.
The oceans, rivers and lakes – all enjoy dining with you.
When you leave, can we follow these tides?
Because they know where you're going,
And only they understand this language you speak;
If I could listen and speak like you, I'd have many friends!
Even if the only word you can say is tranquility, I'd still attend your school.
Let the class begin, because I'm moonlit.

The Seas are Only Tamed by You

They try to run onto land,
But you do not permit them.
You allow them to greet only the sand.
Even for this limited permission – Look, the waves clap!
With the eye of the moon watching, they race to shore;
They all try to rush in before the sun awakens from its nap.
Although they wish they had more,
They sound a happy cry for being allowed to greet land.
As our Creator holds their boundary in his hand,
Give him praise, and fall to your knees,
For He is the only One who can command these seas.
Yes, even though you cheerfully rush in against the sand and rocks,
Jehovah has said: *"**Here is where your proud waves will stop**"*! – JOB 38:1

To a Flamingo

"How beautiful you are, and how pleasant you are,
O beloved girl, above all exquisite delights!"– SONG OF SOLOMON 7:6

Her graceful appearance is like a flamingo
She stands like a ruby colored lamp
Her incurable elegance is a breathtaking pink
From her nourishment is a result of elegance with a rainbow colored mink
The beauty of her elongated legs causes a spectacle
Her direction is a craving for One who narrates her wanderlust
To a flamingo who stands unique,
Whose feathers have been painted with love;
She speaks a tone of quietness, being mild & meek
Her endowed beauty is enshrined with tenderness
Her neck is sleek, yet a supply of pleasure...
Among her companions she is seen with luminous feathers
Her craving for solitude is what makes her special,
because she attends to the secret person of the heart
She is sociable, but seeks solitude from the wild
Like a flamingo is her beauty with character found undeniably mild

GARY FREDERIC

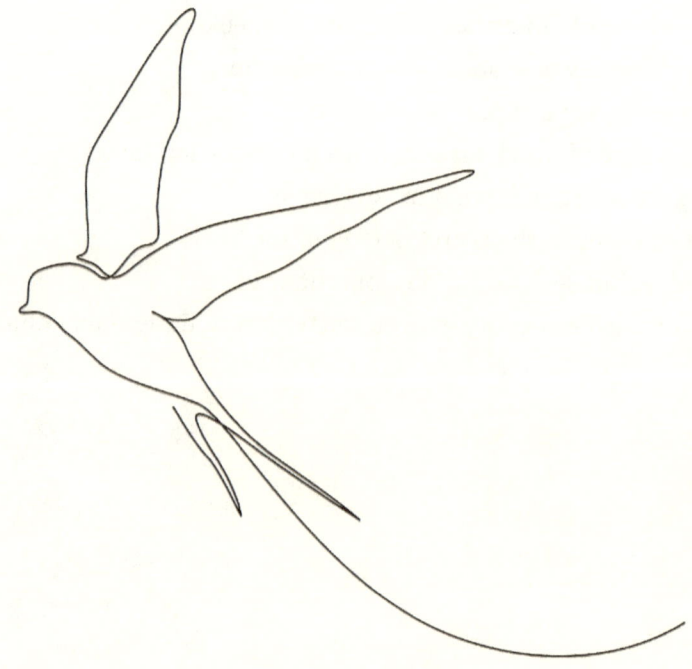

You Don't Need Wings to Fly Higher than Birds

If you had wings,
Where would you go?
If you could fly,
Would you let anyone know?
Like a bird that sings,
Would you dance on the wind?
If it were your way of travel,
Would you fly only to escape?
Would you use it only to flee from battle,
Just from trouble you don't want to face?
Would you go somewhere farther than space?
Or like an eagle,
Would you fly to look down to see everything like a needle?
Or maybe you'd fly as high as you can,
To a place where no man stands.

O, if you had wings to fly,
You'd learn it's not needed to sigh.
Because without wings higher than birds we can fly!
We can reach a throne which they cannot,
Because our Maker gave us a special spot.
No matter what the message we bring,
Remember what the heart can sing.
Our flight can surpass them through prayer!

You Life My Heart Up

Even though you funnel your thoughts to stream
A generous supply is given to help redeem
To purge the rust that slowly creeps in
And foster Truth within
With something that is immutable
You fuse flows which are inimitable
Like a magnet my heart calls out for more
Because it's just the right pulse to score
And it always makes me say
The absolutely right hooray:
'You life my heart up, Jehovah!'

About Gary Frederic

Gary Frederic is a poet and traveler with a deep appreciation for the Creator and His creation. Born to immigrant parents in Brooklyn, NY, Gary grew up in a modest household. Despite their circumstances, his parents were always hospitable and generous, instilling in him a love for learning and helping others. Gary discovered the power of sharing, recognizing that even with limited resources, one can make a positive impact. Over the past thirty years, he has channeled this ethos into writing poetry and literature, aiming to encourage and inspire others.

Having spent twenty-four years in Brooklyn, Gary relocated to the South, where he met his wife. Together, they embarked on extensive travels, immersing themselves in diverse cultures and connecting with local communities. Gary's adventures engaging with elephants in Thailand, going on a Safari in South Africa, cradling endangered turtle species in Sri Lanka, standing alongside kangaroos in Australia, admiring the Swiss Alps from a mountain peak in Switzerland, and enjoying quiet moments at coffee shops in Barcelona, Spain, and Paris, France. These global experiences have deepened Gary's appreciation for cultural diversity and the awe-inspiring wonders of the natural world.

Gary's greatest love is learning about the Creator through the pages of the Bible. He believes that the Bible tells us much about our Creator, just as a novel can tell us much about its author. He also sees God's fingerprint in all of creation. This perspective fuels his joy in writing about the Creator and His creation and engaging in meaningful conversations about spirituality with others. Through his poetry, Gary aspires to kindle inspiration and encourage others to do the same.

GARY FREDERIC

www.ingramcontent.com/pod-product-compliance
Lightning Source LLC
Chambersburg PA
CBHW020921140626
46545CB00015B/1182